KEVIN DURANT

Get in the game with your favorite athletes:

BECKY SAUERBRUNN

TAMBA HALI

KEVIN DURANT

SLOANE STEPHENS

REAL SPORTS
CONTENT NETWORK PRESENTS

KEVIN DURANT

Craig Ellenport

ALADDIN

NEW YORK   LONDON   TORONTO   SYDNEY   NEW DELHI

ALADDIN

An imprint of Simon & Schuster Children's Publishing Division

1230 Avenue of the Americas, New York, New York 10020

First Aladdin paperback edition November 2019

Text copyright © 2019 by Real Sports Content Network Inc.

Cover background photograph copyright © 2019 by WENN Rights Ltd/Alamy Stock Photo

Cover figure photograph copyright © 2019 by Phil Walter/Getty Images

Also available in an Aladdin hardcover edition.

For information about special discounts for bulk purchases, please contact Simon & Schuster Special Sales at 1-866-506-1949 or business@simonandschuster.com.

The Simon & Schuster Speakers Bureau can bring authors to your live event. For more information or to book an event contact the Simon & Schuster Speakers Bureau at 1-866-248-3049 or visit our website at www.simonspeakers.com.

Series designed by Greg Stadnyk

Interior designed by Tom Daly

The text of this book was set in Caecilia LT Std.

Manufactured in the United States of America 1019 OFF

2 4 6 8 10 9 7 5 3 1

Library of Congress Control Number 2019939319

ISBN 978-1-4814-8223-3 (hc)

ISBN 978-1-4814-8222-6 (pbk)

ISBN 978-1-4814-8224-0 (eBook)

CONTENTS

KEVIN DURANT: THE BASICS

BIRTHDAY: September 29, 1988

HOMETOWN: Washington, DC (But he grew up in Prince George's County, Maryland, a town just east of Washington, DC.)

PRIMARY POSITION: Durant plays small forward, and he's one of the best in National Basketball Association (NBA) history at that position. Small forward is perhaps the most versatile position on the basketball court, and the small forward is often the best athlete on the team. Because of his height, coaches sometimes thought of Durant as more of a center or a power forward, since the tallest players usually play those positions. But Durant always preferred to play small forward so that he could do more things, like shoot jumpers farther away from the basket.

CURRENT TEAM: Brooklyn Nets (NBA)

FORMER PROFESSIONAL TEAMS: Seattle SuperSonics (2007–08), Oklahoma City Thunder (2008–16), Golden State Warriors (2016–19)

COLLEGE: University of Texas (2006–07). Kevin decided after his first year of college that he was ready to become a professional basketball player, so he declared himself eligible for the 2007 NBA Draft.

SHORT LIST OF BASKETBALL ACHIEVEMENTS: *High School*: McDonald's All American Game Co-MVP (2006). *College*: Consensus All-American (2007);

Naismith Men's College Player of the Year (2007). *Professional*: Two-time NBA champion (2017 and 2018); two-time NBA Finals MVP (2017 and 2018); NBA Most Valuable Player (2014); four-time NBA scoring champion (2010–12, 2014); nine-time NBA All-Star (2010–18).

US MEN'S NATIONAL TEAM: Gold medal winner and MVP, 2010 International Basketball Federation (known as "FIBA") World Championship; two-time Olympic gold medal winner (London 2012; Rio de Janeiro, 2016); 2010 USA Basketball Male Athlete of the Year; 2016 USA Basketball Male Athlete of the Year (tied with Carmelo Anthony).

GETTING TO THE NBA: On June 28, 2007, Kevin Durant was selected by the Seattle SuperSonics in the NBA Draft. The Portland Trail Blazers had the first pick in the draft and chose Greg Oden from Ohio State University. Durant was the second overall pick.

NICKNAME: Ever since he became a star player in the NBA, Durant has been known simply as "KD." In 2013 a new nickname for Durant started making the rounds. Because of his slender build and the fact that his presence on the court was usually bad news for opponents, fans and broadcasters started calling him "the Slim Reaper." Durant was not a fan of being associated with the grim reaper, also known as the angel of death. When a fan asked him about it on Twitter in early 2014, Durant's reply was, "I like KD better."

HIS MANTRA: "Hard work beats talent when talent fails to work hard." Durant learned this at a young age, and he's never forgotten it. He is quick to correct people who think he was born with a God-given talent, and let them know that he never would have been such a good basketball player without putting in the hard work.

WHAT YOU REALLY NEED TO KNOW ABOUT HIM: Considering how skinny he is, it may come as a surprise to know that Durant eats a lot of candy. "I'm a big Now and Later guy. A Starburst guy," he once confessed. His friends say he's addicted to candy, but Durant doesn't see it as being very unusual. "Doesn't everyone love candy?"

FIRST TITLE

Fifty-five seconds—less than a minute. That's how much time was left in Game 5 of the 2017 NBA Finals, and it was not enough time for the Cleveland Cavaliers to overtake the Golden State Warriors. There would be no miracle comeback this time. Not like the previous year, when Golden State had led Cleveland three games to one, only to see the Cavaliers win three straight games and capture the title.

This time Game 5 was out of reach for the Cavaliers, and it was clear that the Warriors were about to win their second NBA title in three seasons.

Fifty-five seconds, and it would all be over. But Kevin Durant couldn't wait. Overcome with emotion, he went to the half-court line, bent down on one knee, and said to himself, "Is this really happening?"

That's when teammate Andre Iguodala came over to remind Durant that the game wasn't over yet. "Get up!" his teammate shouted. "Keep playing 'til the end!"

What is it that veteran players say about how to properly celebrate?

Act like you've been there before.

But Kevin Durant had not been there before. He hadn't been playing for the Warriors when they'd won the title in 2015. Sure, he had enough individual honors to fill an arena: Rookie of the Year . . . regular-season MVP . . . all-star game MVP . . . eight-time all-star . . . four-time NBA scoring champion . . . Olympic gold medalist.

But Kevin Durant had never been an NBA

champion . . . until those final fifty-five seconds had ticked off the clock at the Oracle Arena in Oakland, California, wrapping up one of the most amazing and dominant playoff runs in NBA history. Before facing Cleveland in the finals, Golden State had swept through the playoffs without losing a single game.

The Warriors had opened the postseason with a first-round matchup against the Portland Trail Blazers. Four-game sweep. Then came the Utah Jazz. Four-game sweep. Surely things would get a little tougher when they faced the mighty San Antonio Spurs in the Western Conference Finals. Maybe, but the result was the same: four-game sweep.

Durant found himself in the NBA Finals for the second time in his career. Five years earlier, in 2012, he'd helped the Oklahoma City Thunder reach the finals, only to lose in five games to the Miami Heat. That series marked the first NBA championship for another superstar—LeBron James. It set off a chain of events that will forever link James and Durant.

That 2012 title was the first of three NBA championships for James. He won again with the Heat in 2013. The Heat was back in the finals a year later, but they lost to the Spurs. Before the 2014–15 season, James was a free agent. He shocked the NBA universe by returning to the Cleveland Cavaliers, the team he'd played with for his first seven years in the league. He led the Cavaliers to the NBA Finals that season, only to lose to the Warriors. But when the Cavaliers and Warriors met again in the NBA Finals in 2016, James would not be denied.

And that's where Durant comes in. The 2015–16 Golden State Warriors finished the regular season with a record of 73–9, the best single-season record for any team in NBA history. With a roster that included all-stars such as Stephen Curry, Klay Thompson, and Draymond Green, the Warriors were almost unbeatable. And yet the Cavaliers pulled off the upset, coming back from a 3–1 deficit to take the title in seven games and bring an NBA championship to the city of Cleveland for the first time ever.

After the Warriors lost in the finals, most NBA experts predicted that the team would be a force in the 2016–17 season and have a good chance to get to their third straight NBA Finals with the existing lineup, which had just won seventy-three regular-season games.

But the Warriors were not content to cruise into the next season without improving their lineup. And they did so with a bang.

Durant was the most coveted free agent following the 2015–16 season. He and Russell Westbrook were the foundation of an Oklahoma City Thunder team that had been to the NBA Finals in 2012 and had been up three games to one against the Warriors in the 2016 Western Conference Finals, only to see the Warriors come back and win. Many fans hoped Durant would re-sign with the Thunder.

On July 4, 2016, Durant wrote a story for the Players' Tribune website, announcing his decision:

"The primary mandate I had for myself in making this decision was to have it based on the potential for my growth as a player—as that has always steered me in the right direction," Durant wrote. "But I am also at a point in my life where it is of equal importance to find an opportunity that encourages my evolution as a man: moving out of my comfort zone to a new city and community which offers the greatest potential for my contribution and personal growth. With this in mind, I have decided that I am going to join the Golden State Warriors."

Durant's decision was met with much criticism. Why would he sign with a team that was already loaded with talent and didn't really need another superstar?

Durant spent a lot of time talking about that subject, since he was asked about it almost everywhere he went during the 2016–17 season. But when those final seconds ran down in Game 5 of the NBA Finals, Durant got the only answer he needed.

For the first time in his career, he was an NBA champion. Not only that—Durant was named the NBA Finals MVP.

Durant continued to hear from his detractors that he had taken the easy way out by joining the Warriors. Many of the things people were saying about him were pretty hurtful. But Durant had the ability to drown out what he called "the noise."

He had been through much worse in his life. It wasn't as if he'd been able to do whatever he wanted when he was a kid. The young Kevin Durant had worked tirelessly and had earned all the achievements and accolades that would come.

CHAPTER 2

PG COUNTY

It's easy to see all that Kevin Durant has now and be a little jealous.

Money? He gets paid millions of dollars to play basketball for a living, and companies pay him to be their pitchman. Heck, he's got his own sneaker line.

Fame? He's got his own YouTube channel, with nearly seven hundred thousand subscribers. On Twitter he's got more than seventeen million followers.

Okay, but don't think that Kevin Durant has always had a charmed life. Before the fame and before the money, he was a skinny kid growing up in a place where just staying out of trouble was considered a success. His early years were spent in a broken family that was often struggling to make ends meet. While his height has been a great advantage in his career, it was something he was self-conscious about as a kid. And just as he was becoming a nationally recognized high school star, he was faced with the tragic death of someone very close to him.

Nothing came easily to Durant, but it is the challenges of his youth and the lessons learned that have helped him maintain an uncanny work ethic. It is that work ethic that has gotten Durant where he is today.

Kevin Durant was born in Washington, DC, but he grew up in Prince George's County, Maryland, a suburb just east of Washington. PG County, as it's called by the locals, is one of the biggest counties in the state of Maryland . . . and it's also one of the most dangerous. Throughout Durant's childhood, PG County statistically had the highest crime rate in the state.

Making matters worse, he grew up in a tough neighborhood without a father.

Durant was born three years after his older brother, Tony. Kevin would later have another brother, Rayvonne, and a sister, Briana. However, something he did not have as a young boy was a father. His dad, Wayne Pratt, left the family before Durant's first birthday. Wayne lived and worked in the area. He would see his boys now and then, and he provided child support to Wanda, Kevin's mother. But he wasn't a steady presence in Kevin's early years.

That left Wanda Durant with the burden of being a single parent. She got plenty of help from her mother—Kevin's grandmother—Barbara Davis, but it was Wanda who was the rock of the family. She worked tirelessly to provide for her children.

Wanda worked the night shift at the post office while Barbara took care of the kids. She wanted to provide a better life for her children, and she knew that a strong work ethic was what they needed. Wanda led by example, and made sure that Kevin and his brother Tony both grew up understanding that hard work could pay off.

But nothing came easily. The family—Kevin, his mother, and his brother—moved often, struggling to find an apartment or small house with a rent they could afford. Despite all the moving, Durant said he felt like he was in a box that he couldn't escape.

Part of that was the fear of not knowing what was around the corner. You had to watch your back, as Durant said. There were gangs and territories, and you had to be careful where you were going and who you were talking to.

It helped that Kevin had a big brother who was always looking out for his little bro. Kevin and Tony did everything together when they were kids. They kept busy after school by playing sports at the local Boys & Girls Club. Like any siblings, they fought from time to time, but they had each other's backs.

A perfect example of the boys fighting—and helping—each other occurred when Kevin was in the eighth grade.

Things got particularly nasty one day, and Kevin threw a boot at his brother's head. Tony ducked out of the way, and the boot struck a glass light-switch cover on the wall, shattering the glass. Kevin didn't have the money to fix what he had broken. Even though they had just been fighting, Tony—who was a high school sophomore at the time and had a part-time job working at McDonald's—loaned Kevin the ten dollars he needed to buy a new light-switch cover.

(When Kevin was a rookie in the NBA, he finally paid his brother back—with interest. He bought Tony a new car.)

Kevin had the love of his family, and he also enjoyed time with his friends. One of his best friends as a kid was Michael Beasley, who amazingly went on to play in the NBA just like Durant did.

"I tell people all the time," Beasley told ESPN.com, "when you a kid, you don't know you're in the hood or you don't know you're poor. You just accepting your environment when you a child, and that's when your friends are really your friends, wholeheartedly and nothing malicious."

Beasley considered Durant his first real friend. Beasley would bring his Xbox with him and have sleepovers at Durant's house. And, of course, they played basketball.

Lots of basketball.

"We hooped everywhere and we didn't care," Durant told ESPN.com. "That's when I started to realize we were friends. I was always in the gym, either by myself or with Mike or with my team."

Because Durant and Beasley both moved around

so much, the basketball court was really the only place where they made friends.

"Every year I'd move," recalled Beasley. "We'd move to different apartments. We lived in every part of PG County. So it was like we didn't really have no stable friends or stable household. Moms was at work. Pops wasn't there. We were just hooping. The people we was around all the time was just us."

It wasn't only basketball that the boys played. Sometimes it would be football. One day Wanda Durant was watching football practice and witnessed what she still loves to bring up as an example of her son's big heart.

The team was running one-on-one tackling drills. The team would form a circle around two players, whose mission it was to take each other down. With the rest of the team cheering them on, the two players would charge at each other, and the first one to hit the ground would lose the drill. It was Durant's turn, and he was matched up against this one particularly small kid who never came out on top in these drills. As the team circled around the two players, the coach looked at the little kid and said, "If you can't take Kevin down, we're all gonna jump on you."

To Wanda's surprise, the kid charged toward Kevin, and sure enough the smaller kid brought Kevin down. After practice Kevin said, "Mom, he couldn't knock me down. I let him tackle me because I didn't want him to get hurt."

"That's the kind of guy Kevin has always been," recalled Wanda.

CHAPTER 3

THE REC CENTER

Since Wanda Durant worked the night shift at the post office, Kevin's grandmother would pick him up from school every day and fix him a peanut butter and jelly sandwich while his mom got some much needed sleep.

Wanda was there for Kevin and Tony in the afternoon and evening, fixing them dinner every night before leaving for work. But Wanda also knew that as her boys were getting older, they needed something to keep them busy after school. When Kevin was about eight years old, a friend of Wanda's told her about the Seat Pleasant Activity Center.

Seat Pleasant is a small city within Prince George's County, and it's where the Durants lived at the time. Wanda couldn't afford to send Kevin and Tony to any after-school programs that cost money. Fortunately for her and her boys, the Seat Pleasant Activity Center was free for residents.

Located on Addison Road in Seat Pleasant, the activity center is a safe haven for kids and a way to keep them busy and off the streets. Known simply as "the rec center," the facility features a gym, a game room, a multipurpose room with couches and a TV, a kitchen, and—most important—a basketball court.

The rec center is where Durant's basketball journey formally began.

"My mom, I think she just wanted to get me and my brother out of the house for a few hours," recalled Durant later. "When I walked into the gym, I fell in love with the game."

Durant was a tall, skinny kid, and he had plenty to learn about the game of basketball.

Fortunately for Durant, there was a coach at Seat Pleasant Activity Center named Charles Craig. It was Craig who taught Durant the basics. More important, he helped Durant believe in himself. As Durant once explained to ESPN, Craig "gave me confidence when I didn't have confidence in myself."

Craig was more than a coach. He was a father figure—not only to Kevin but also to Tony and all the other boys and girls who spent time at the rec center. He made sure they kept up with their schoolwork. If they needed money to buy a soda, he was there. Coach Craig even took Kevin and his brother to the movies on occasion.

But the main thing for Durant was always basketball.

As young Kevin continued to play basketball at the rec center and get better and better, he came to a conclusion. The skinny eight-year-old marched into his mother's room one day and said, "Mom, I want to be an NBA player when I grow up."

"You sure?" Wanda asked. Kevin immediately said yes.

"Well," his mother said, "then we're gonna put the work in."

That's exactly what Durant did, spending several hours every day practicing at Seat Pleasant Activity Center. He could often be found napping somewhere in the back of the gym between practice sessions. "I was always in the gym," Durant once said. "People would look at me crazy because I spent so much time there."

The combination of hard work and natural talent helped Durant improve his game at a rapid pace. It didn't hurt that he continued to grow. Durant was six feet tall in middle school. When he started playing for an Amateur Athletic Union (AAU) team, he was almost always the tallest player on the court.

Playing AAU basketball was a big step. The AAU

is a nationwide organization that includes a wide variety of sports, but it's most closely associated with basketball. Teams travel around the country, and the competition can be fierce. At the highest level of AAU basketball, it's not uncommon to see college recruiters and even NBA scouts in the stands checking out the most talented players.

Durant played AAU for the Prince George's Jaguars, a team coached by Taras Brown. It didn't take long for Brown to see that he had a special player on his hands.

"He works hard, he loves the game, he's a team player," Brown said. "Those are the guys I like to work with."

Because Durant was the tallest kid on the court, he always played center—the anchor who plays under the basket, blocking shots and grabbing rebounds.

Brown saw something different, however. He realized that Durant was faster and quicker than most kids his size. And he had good instincts. What Brown loved the most about Durant's game was that he was always around the ball. Wherever the ball was, that's where Durant was. That was a gift, Brown told his new star pupil.

"So most people saw him as a skinny center who may not be able to do that much," recalled Brown. "Early on, I told Kevin, 'You're not going to be a center. You're too skinny, so we're gonna work on perimeter skills next year. You're gonna play center this year, but next year I'm gonna move you out to the wing.'"

Playing wing meant moving away from the basket, playing shooting guard or small forward. In both cases it required more skill in all facets of the game—dribbling, passing, and shooting. The experience made Durant a more well-rounded player, and he would soon become a force to be reckoned with.

Despite his obvious talent, the key to his success

was that great work ethic and willingness to constantly learn and improve.

One major rule Brown had for Durant: no pickup games. While most of his friends would choose sides and play games of three-on-three or five-on-five basketball all day, there was none of that for Durant. Brown thought pickup games were too disorganized and would mess with Durant's fundamentals. Instead Brown focused on drills. Ball-handling drills. Shooting drills. Dribbling with both hands. Defensive footwork. It wasn't exciting, and it certainly wasn't as much fun as a pickup game, but Durant understood that this was what he needed to do in order to get to the next level.

Brown called it the gift of "want it bad."

"He always wanted to know what he could do better," Brown recalled. "He was more worried about giving it his all, making sure he was doing everything right. And never wanting to leave the court. His practices were the same way. He was a sponge in practice as well as on the court. Even on his off-days, he was contacting me about something about basketball."

As long as Durant was willing to work hard, Brown was happy to do his part and work him as hard as he could. When this wasn't taking place in the gym, it was done outside the rec center—to be specific, on the corner of L Street and Balsamtree Drive. To Durant, this place was simply known as "the Hill."

Brown took him to the Hill often, and made Durant run up the steepest stretch of L Street and then walk back down backward. Over and over again.

When Brown wasn't available, Wanda would take Kevin to the Hill. She would make him run up the Hill twenty-five times. While he was chugging away, Wanda would sit in her car at the bottom of the hill reading a book. Years later Wanda confessed that sometimes she would make Kevin do it twenty-five more times so that she could keep reading.

In 2013, Durant gave local media a tour of his old neighborhood, and he was especially proud to show them the Hill.

"I know when I have a son and he wants to play basketball, this is the first place I'm gonna send him," said Durant. "I'm going to sit in my car and read a book and make him do twenty-five extra like I did. I'm looking forward to that day."

When Durant wasn't doing drills or running hills, Brown would give him homework—make him read books about basketball or watch videos. Brown made him watch highlight after highlight of Larry Bird, the Hall of Fame forward for the Boston Celtics. Bird was one of the greatest shooters in NBA history.

"We studied Larry Bird," Brown later explained. "I would say, 'Watch what he does. Watch the little things he does.' And he picked it up right away. Started doing some of those things on the court without realizing he was doing it. My favorite line to him at that time was, 'You can't be it unless you see it.'

"So if you're watching him, you're going to emulate, imitate what you see. Your mind is going to do it for you. That's what I used to make him do. Give him homework. Watch Larry Bird."

All the hard work paid off. When he was eleven years old, Durant led the PG Jaguars to an AAU national championship. Playing with his good friend Michael Beasley and another future NBA player, Chris Braswell, Durant scored eighteen points in the second half of the championship game, which was played in Orlando, Florida. Durant later called it his fondest childhood memory.

"Probably the best feeling I had up until that point," he once said.

That was actually the first of two AAU national championships that the Jaguars won with Durant. Taras Brown had coached plenty of excellent basketball players through the years, but it was clear that none had been as talented as Durant.

As the years passed, Brown became much more than a coach to Durant. The two became very close, and Brown eventually was named Durant's godfather. Since the day they met, Brown has been a big influence on Durant in all aspects of life—and he remains a big part of Durant's life to this day.

"At a young age, he never wanted to disappoint anybody," Brown said of Durant. "He was willing to do whatever you asked him, and he had those natural gifts where people liked to be around him. They wanted to play for him, they wanted to play with him. And he seemed to make everybody around him feel better. And that's the type of traits you have to have in today's society."

Perhaps Brown's favorite story that describes just how much Durant cared about everyone around him occurred when the Jaguars were playing an AAU game in Memphis, Tennessee. They were playing a team from Cincinnati, and Durant was having one of those typical Kevin Durant games. No matter where he was shooting from, he just couldn't miss.

"I think he had about twenty-five at the half," Brown recalled. "The coaches are saying, 'He's on fire. We've got to keep feeding him.' Kevin comes over to us and says, 'Hey, I would like to sit down in the second half. Let them play.'"

The team was comfortably ahead, and he wanted some of his teammates who were sitting on the bench to get into the game and have some fun. And since Durant often scored big and gave his team huge leads, he did this all the time.

"He was never one of those players who said, 'I need to play, score this many points. I need to be in the game,'" said Brown. "He always wanted his teammates to share in his success as well as theirs. Many times he would take himself out.

"He might even fake an injury to let his friend play—'Oh, my stomach hurts.' I knew what he was doing."

CHAPTER **4**

TRAGEDY STRIKES

Tony Durant was a pretty good basketball player in his own right. The two brothers never played on the same team, though. By the time Kevin was set to go to high school, Tony had already moved on. He had played for the Suitland High School basketball team as a freshman, when Kevin was still in middle school. But then Tony decided he wanted to try something new. He transferred to St. John's Military School in Salina, Kansas.

Tony would be home during the summers, but for the most part Kevin and Wanda were on their own—though not entirely. Wayne Pratt, the boys' father, was back in the picture. He was there more often, for both Kevin and Wanda. He drove Kevin to practices and games and went on the road with him for AAU tournaments. And by 2001 he would be reunited with Wanda.

For the first time Kevin Durant felt as if he were part of an average American family. Just in time to begin his high school years. But he didn't go to Suitland, his local public school.

The basketball coach at National Christian Academy in Fort Washington, Maryland, had seen Durant play as an eighth grader. He'd been so impressed that he'd offered Kevin a scholarship to play at the private school. So that's where Durant began his high school career.

Midway through Durant's freshman year, the coach bumped him up to the varsity team. Everyone could see that he was a major talent. Problem was, the returning players on the team felt threatened. They did not welcome Durant to the team with open arms. In fact, they went out of their way to shun him. In practices and in games, they ignored him and made a point not to pass him the ball.

Durant was very upset about this. He felt like quitting, and he almost did. But he knew that quitting wasn't an option. He thought about all the hard work and sacrifices that his mom had made to give him the chance to play basketball. He thought about all the work he'd done with Taras Brown, trying to be the best he could be on the court. He thought about Charles Craig, who'd given him a chance at the rec center and had been a father figure to him when his real father hadn't been around.

Durant put his head down and just kept working. His AAU teammates knew that Durant wasn't in it for himself. He was always a team-first player. Amazingly, those unwelcoming high school teammates eventually came to see that Durant just wanted to win as a team.

To no one's surprise, once they allowed Durant to be part of the team, success followed.

By the end of the year, Durant had established himself as a high school star, and basketball fans filled the gym to watch his games.

By the end of his second season at National Christian Academy, even more people began to take notice. The *Washington Post* named him the area Player of the Year.

After two years at National Christian Academy, it was clear to everyone that Durant had a bright future that could eventually see him playing in the NBA. For that reason his support team—his parents, Taras Brown, Charles Craig—all agreed that he should be playing at a school that could get him more national attention. Durant transferred to Oak Hill Academy, a school in Virginia that was three hundred sixty miles from home. The reason?

Oak Hill Academy is known as an elite basketball school. It had produced NBA stars such as Carmelo Anthony and Jerry Stackhouse, so Oak Hill was a good place for Durant to get the attention of major college programs and the NBA.

Despite the distance from home, Durant wasn't alone when he got to Oak Hill. One of his teammates was another Prince George's County resident and an AAU teammate—Ty Lawson.

Durant enjoyed his time at Oak Hill. But in the spring of that year, something happened back home that would change his life forever.

Kevin and his brother Tony were among the lucky ones growing up in PG County. They received love and support, and managed to avoid the streets and stay out of trouble. In some parts of PG County, however, staying out of trouble can be impossible even if one's intentions are good.

On April 30, 2005, Charles Craig—Durant's coach, mentor, and father figure from Seat Pleasant

Activity Center—tried to break up a brawl that had erupted outside a local bar. Craig had been there with some family and friends, who tried to keep Craig from getting involved. As Durant later put it, Craig was in the wrong place at the wrong time.

One of the men who had been fighting had a gun. Craig was shot four times. He died in the parking lot.

The irony was more than tragic. Craig had been responsible for keeping Durant and so many other kids off the streets. He'd showed them that there was more to life, that anything was possible for those who worked hard and lived right. All the time that Durant had spent with Craig at the rec center had been pivotal in his development as a basketball player. But it had been even more important for his development as a person. Having a mentor like Charles Craig to keep Durant focused had helped him stay positive.

"He loved kids," Charles Craig's mother, Claudette Craig, said years after the murder. "He would do anything for any child. He had a van, and he'd come by with a bunch of kids and say, 'Ma, I got a bunch of hungry kids, can you feed 'em?' I'd say, 'If you get the food, I'll cook it.' He was a terrible cook."

So many people came to pay their respects at Craig's funeral that people who drove by the church must have thought that the service was for a political dignitary or someone else who'd been very important. In fact, Craig *had been* very important to a lot of people, most notably the kids of Seat Pleasant.

So it was understandable that Durant was devastated when he heard the news that Craig had been murdered in a random act of violence.

"I thought he was like Superman," Durant told ESPN. "I didn't think anything would happen to him. To hear that, to hear that he wasn't going to be around anymore, I was shocked."

Durant's shock turned to anger, and that anger

about losing his mentor started to show itself on the basketball court. He started trash-talking and fouling more. He was playing erratically, and everyone could see it.

Fortunately for Durant, he had a strong support system. With the help of his loved ones, he decided to leave Oak Hill Academy to be closer to home. Durant played his senior year of high school at Montrose Christian School in Rockville, Maryland.

Montrose Christian was only thirty-five miles from home, much closer than Oak Hill. It might not have been the NBA factory that Oak Hill was, but that wasn't Durant's priority now.

One thing that was heavy on Durant's mind: he wanted to do something to honor his first basketball coach. After talking it over with his godfather, he decided he would wear jersey number thirty-five—that was Craig's age when he died.

Durant wore number thirty-five when he went to college at the University of Texas, and he's been number thirty-five in the NBA. When he sees fans all around the country wearing his jersey, he fondly remembers the man who meant so much to him.

He even started a trend back in Seat Pleasant, encouraging kids who got their start at the rec center to wear number thirty-five jerseys when they went on to high school and college ball. Kevin's brother Tony wore thirty-five when he played at Towson University. Chris Braswell, who became a star college player at the University of North Carolina at Charlotte, also wore number thirty-five in honor of Craig.

"It feels good to see a lot of thirty-fives from the people I know," Durant said. "It shows that every time we step between the lines, where he taught us how to be tough, how to go out there and play with passion and play with heart, even though he's up there, he's living his dreams through us on the basketball court."

CHAPTER 5

ONE AND DONE

Durant was back home for his senior year of high school, but Montrose Christian wasn't a local school. It was about an hour-long commute by train. Still, Durant got up early every morning and was at school by seven thirty in order to squeeze in some basketball practice before class.

By the time he got to Montrose, Durant had grown five inches and stood at six feet, seven inches. But it wasn't just his size that helped Durant dominate. With his focus and work ethic back on track, he had an outstanding senior year.

He led the Montrose Christian School Mustangs to a 20–2 record, averaging twenty-four points, ten rebounds, three assists, and three steals per game. His last game for the Mustangs was a classic matchup against the number-one-ranked team in the country—which happened to be the Oak Hill Academy Warriors, his former team. Durant scored a game-high thirty-one points as Montrose Christian ended Oak Hill's fifty-six-game winning streak. Montrose finished as the nation's number two team, according to *USA Today*.

By the time his senior year was over, Durant was undeniably one of the top high school players in the country. The coach at Montrose was Stu Vetter, who had a national reputation and was well connected with prominent college basketball coaches. That definitely helped get Durant's name out there.

Durant was named the Washington Post All-Met Player of the Year. In the newspaper's write-up they said Durant had "remarkable agility and skills for a player so tall."

As one of the best high school players in the country, Durant was invited to play in the McDonald's All American Game at the end of the season. Started in the late 1970s, the McDonald's All American Game routinely features future NBA stars. Hall of Famers such as Magic Johnson, Michael Jordan, and Shaquille O'Neal, just to name a few, were all chosen to participate.

Durant not only added his name to that roster of talent—he was named co-MVP of the game.

When he graduated from high school, Durant was widely considered the second-rated high school basketball prospect in the entire country.

"He could've played for us on Friday night and played for the [NBA Washington] Wizards on Sunday," said Vetter, his coach. "And he was only seventeen at the time. He was that talented."

Durant's dream of playing in the NBA was so

close that he could taste it. If he'd had his way, he would have followed in the footsteps of superstars such as LeBron James and Kobe Bryant, who were so talented that they went straight from high school to the pros. Unfortunately for Durant, he was a year too late for that.

In 2005 the NBA and its players' union made a deal. The new rule was that a player had to be at least nineteen years old and be out of high school for at least one year before entering the NBA Draft.

"I think I would have gone this year if I could have, because that's my dream, to go to the NBA," Durant told the *New York Times* in the spring of 2006. "Why not sooner than later?"

With the new rule in place, it was believed that the best young basketball players in the country would play in college for one year and then leave school to enter the NBA Draft. "One and done," it would be called.

Durant didn't rule out the possibility of staying

in college longer—and his mother really wanted him to graduate—but "one and done" was definitely on his mind. Now the question was: Where would he go to college?

Of course, as one of the top-ranked high school players in the country, big-time college basketball schools had been contacting Durant back when he was still at Oak Hill Academy. Two of the schools that Durant was interested in playing for were the University of North Carolina and the University of Connecticut. North Carolina and Connecticut were both members of the Atlantic Coast Conference (ACC), which was close to home, and both schools were among the strongest basketball powerhouses in the country. Even if he only stayed in college for one year, why not play for a team that could win the national championship?

Ty Lawson, his childhood friend from PG County, pushed hard to get Durant to join him at North Carolina. Lawson and Durant had been teammates at Oak Hill Academy, and both had been named high school All-Americans. Lawson thought they would make a dynamic duo playing for the North Carolina Tar Heels, a perennial basketball power-house that had just won the school's sixth national championship in 2005.

It was tempting.

But there was one other school that interested Durant, a good basketball school but not as good as North Carolina or Connecticut—and not as close, either.

The University of Texas.

As a matter of fact, the University of Texas had been the first college to show an interest in Durant. Back when he'd been a sophomore at the National Christian Academy, Kevin had been play-ing in a tournament in Delaware. Texas assistant coach Russell Springmann was there—to scout a different player on a different team. Springmann later told the *Austin American-Statesman* that when he saw Durant hit a three-point shot from the corner, he took notice. The recruiting process was under way.

Coach Springmann told his head coach, Rick Barnes, about Durant. You've got to see him yourself, Springmann said. Coach Barnes was sold the first time he saw Durant play, and every time Barnes saw Durant play after that, he could see improvement.

At the end of his junior year at Oak Hill Academy, Durant made his official recruiting trip to the University of Texas. Durant's dad went with him, and that night the two had a steak dinner with Springmann and Barnes. When Wayne Pratt saw the way Durant was laughing with Coach Barnes, he knew Texas was the right school for his son. Later that summer Durant signed a letter of intent to go to Austin, Texas, to play for the University of Texas Longhorns.

When a high school athlete announces what

college he'll be attending, it's called a "commitment." Make no mistake about it, choosing to go from PG County, Maryland, to Austin, Texas, was quite a commitment. The University of Texas was more than fifteen hundred miles from the place that Durant had always called home. It was a three-and-a-half-hour plane ride—and that was if you could book a nonstop flight, which wasn't easy.

But Durant was ready for the challenge. Playing AAU basketball, traveling to big tournaments, and playing in prestigious high school all-star games had prepared him for this. He was ready for the new adventure in Texas.

What he didn't know was that his comfort and ease around Coach Barnes wasn't the only reason why Wayne and Wanda liked the idea of their son playing for Texas. No, they had thought this all through pretty carefully—and they'd done their research.

Years later they admitted their strategy to

Coach Springmann. They thought the most import-ant thing that Durant needed to grow as a player was to be put into a leadership role. He was always the best player on the court, but he needed to be a better leader, they thought.

At North Carolina that wouldn't have happened, at least not right away. The Tar Heels were coming off a national championship season, and they had several returning players who'd been part of that title run and were used to playing high-pressure games.

The University of Texas, meanwhile, would be in serious need of new leadership when Durant got there in the fall of 2006. The Longhorns had won a school-record thirty games the previous season, and they'd made it to the quarterfinals—the Elite Eight—of the NCAA Tournament. But three players from that team—LaMarcus Aldridge, P. J. Tucker, and Daniel Gibson—went on to the NBA after that season.

When Durant got to Texas, he joined a twelve-man roster that consisted of seven freshman, two sophomores, two juniors, and just one senior. Clearly the Longhorns were a young team in need of new leadership. Just as Durant's parents had mapped out.

When he began playing for Texas in the fall of 2006, it took no time at all for Durant to make a major impact. In his very first college game, he scored twenty points against Alcorn State. At the time it was a new freshman record at the school. That record would be shattered many more times by Durant before the season was over. He scored at least twenty points in thirty games, including thirty-seven points in a game, twice. He led the entire Big 12 Conference in scoring (more than twenty-five points per game), rebounding (more than eleven rebounds per game), blocked shots (sixty-seven), and double-doubles—games with at least ten points and at least ten rebounds (twenty).

He was the only player in the country to rank in the top ten in both scoring and rebounding. (He ranked fourth in both categories.)

"His growth as a player was amazing," Springmann told SiriusXM's Mad Dog Sports Radio. "Coach Barnes did an incredible job with Kevin."

Springmann recalled a day late in the season when Barnes was talking to reporters about Durant. By then it was clear that Durant was perhaps the best freshman player in all of college basketball. Barnes thought maybe that wasn't enough.

Barnes told reporters that day that the media needed to look at Durant as more than the freshman of the year but as the player of the year.

"He was that good," said Springmann. "And that was something that we all believed, that Kevin had the ability to be the best player in the country."

For Durant, his freshman season at college was a major breakthrough. Not that he hadn't already known he was good. But the one thing that Durant had lacked when he was younger was confidence.

"When I didn't play well, my confidence always took a hit," he recalled. "It was always up and down. So I didn't really know until I got to college and I was just like, 'Yeah, I'm better than him. . . . He can't check me. . . . He can't stop me.'

"I started to gain that confidence, then after a while I'm like, 'Oh, this will be a reality right here, this is my life now.'"

Sure enough, Durant received the 2007 John R. Wooden Award as college basketball's most outstanding player. The award had first been presented in 1977, and this was the first time it was won by a freshman.

Durant led the Longhorns to a 25–10 record and on a trip to the second round of the NCAA Tournament.

Not only did Durant improve his basketball skills that first year at Texas, but he also improved as a leader—just as his parents had planned.

"They knew Kevin would be thrust into a leadership position immediately, and it was going to be great for him," said Coach Springmann. "And it was. He grew as a young man. He grew as a leader."

Now Durant had the talent, the work ethic, the leadership, and a year of college experience. It was time to realize his dream.

On April 10, 2007, Durant announced that he would enter the NBA Draft.

Before he announced it to the public, there was the matter of telling Coach Barnes about his decision. Most people—Barnes included—had expected this to happen, but Durant still felt a little guilty anyway.

"The day that he walked into my room, he cried," Barnes recalled. "He said, 'Coach, I don't really know how to say it, but I think it's time to pursue the draft.' And he had to. One, he should have been the very first pick. I mean, that was a no-brainer. He wasn't, but it didn't matter. You just knew wherever he went, he was going to be a difference maker."

The thing is, Durant was a difference maker on and off the court. He made a positive impression on almost everyone he came into contact with.

It was obvious that he'd made a big impression on Coach Springmann.

After the Longhorns lost to the University of Southern California in the second round of the 2007 NCAA Tournament—which would be Durant's last game for Texas—Springmann was talking to Kevin's mom.

"I want to thank you guys, because I've learned a lot from your son," Springmann said.

Wanda asked what he meant.

"To be honest with you," the coach said, "I learned that it's all right to tell another man that you love him. That's one of the things that your son taught me. Because Kevin would tell you, 'I love you.' . . . For a lot of men, that could be an awkward thing to say, and Kevin would easily express himself. That's just one example, and I could give you a million."

A few years later Springmann did something that proved just how much he thought of Durant. Springmann named his first son after Durant.

How did Springmann's wife feel about naming her son Durant Springmann?

"She loved it," the coach said. "We wouldn't have just flippantly decided, 'That's a cool name.' It's about who he is."

When they had decided to name the baby after Durant, Springmann called Wanda to let her know. "If our son is half the person that your son is," he told her, "we would be amazingly blessed."

Springmann added: "Kevin's one of the best people that I've ever been around. Not one of the best young people, one of the best people I've ever had the pleasure of knowing. I just respect who he is as a man. He's got strong character, and he's got a tremendous work ethic, and he's got a huge heart."

Kevin Durant wasn't the only player to enter the 2007 NBA Draft after his freshman season of college. The NBA had just adopted the rule stating that players had to be at least nineteen years old and out of high school for a year before entering the draft. So it's entirely possible that a bunch of freshmen standouts from around the nation had been hoping to skip college altogether. That was something Durant had thought about, after all.

Greg Oden, a freshman from Ohio State University, was the first overall pick in the draft. When Durant was taken second, it marked the first time in NBA history that the first two players drafted were freshmen.

But the trend didn't stop there. Five of the first ten draft picks were freshmen. Overall, eight of the thirty first-round picks were freshmen—only three freshmen were drafted in the first round in the previous two years combined. Comparatively, only six of the thirty were seniors. Eight were juniors, three were sophomores, and five were international players who had not attended US colleges.

Ten years later, "one and done" is more commonplace than ever. In the 2017 NBA Draft, a record sixteen freshmen were taken in the first round—including ten of the top eleven picks.

In any case, Durant was finally on his way to the NBA. Little did he know, his new home was not going to be home for long.

CHAPTER 6

MVP MOM

Durant was drafted by the Seattle SuperSonics. By now he was used to traveling far from PG County to play basketball, but Seattle was just about as far from Maryland as possible without leaving the country altogether. Located in the northwest corner of the United States, Seattle was nearly three thousand miles from home.

Durant would have a solid support team around him—his SuperSonics teammates, his coaches, and a professional organization helping him to get acclimated to life in the NBA.

Chances are that he would have been fine on his own, but Wanda Durant wouldn't have any part of that. Her son was just nineteen years old, and she wanted to look out for him. So she got time off her job at the post office and moved out to Seattle with him.

It didn't take long for Durant to make his mark in the NBA. In his first regular-season game as a pro, he finished with eighteen points, five rebounds, and three steals. By the time his first season was over, he'd become just the third teenager in league history to average at least twenty points per game. The others were Carmelo Anthony and LeBron James—elite company. For his efforts, Durant was named 2008 NBA Rookie of the Year.

As it turned out, that was the end of Durant's time in Seattle. Not just Durant, actually—the entire team. The SuperSonics relocated to Oklahoma City, Oklahoma, with a new name: the Thunder.

It was a new team, but the same Durant. As

he had done throughout his youth when it came to basketball, Durant continued to work hard and continued to get better and better. As the seasons passed, he became an NBA superstar. He was a perennial selection for the all-star game, and four times he led the league in scoring.

Of course, Wanda Durant followed her son from Seattle to Oklahoma City. She didn't live there permanently—her sons had bought her a house back in Maryland—but she was a regular fixture at Thunder home games. As the Thunder became one of the best teams in the NBA, fans grew accustomed to seeing Kevin get a hug and kiss from Wanda after a big win.

Mama's boy?

Most NBA players would not want to be called that. Kevin Durant is fine with it.

Wanda Durant was just twenty-one years old when Kevin was born—and he was the second child she would have to care for while trying to work enough to keep food on the table.

"There were many nights that I didn't know how we were going to make it," she told CBS News years later.

For all the hard work and sacrifice that Wanda had put into helping her children thrive, Kevin was more than happy to make sure she enjoyed the spoils of his success.

If there was ever a question of just how much Durant loved and appreciated his mom, it was answered when he made his acceptance speech after winning the NBA MVP following the 2013–14 season. Durant was emotional throughout the speech as he thanked everyone from his teammates to the Thunder organization to his family. He saved his mom for last, and spoke from the heart about the sacrifices she'd made as a single mom working to give her children a chance to succeed:

"And last, my mom," he said. "I don't think you know what you did. You had my brother when you were eighteen years old. Three years later, I came out. The odds were stacked against us. Single parent with two boys by the time you were twenty-one years old. Everybody told us we weren't supposed to be here. We went from apartment to apartment by ourselves. One of the best memories I had was when we moved into our first apartment, no bed, no furniture, and we just sat in the living room and just hugged each other. We thought we made it.

"We weren't supposed to be here," Durant continued, addressing his mother. "You made us believe. You kept us off the street. You put clothes on our backs. You put food on the table. When you didn't eat, you made sure we ate and [you] went to sleep hungry. You sacrificed for us.

"You're the real MVP."

Kevin was crying. Wanda was crying. And so were many others in attendance.

"I was expecting him to mention me, of course, but I didn't think it would be to that magnitude, and I didn't think he'd remember some of the events of our past, and how it would resonate with him," Wanda said after the speech. "So I was a little overwhelmed with the emotion, and I reflected on the things we had come through as a family."

Durant's speech didn't make just SportsCenter that night. It was replayed on news broadcasts around the country and went viral on the Internet. People who didn't even watch basketball suddenly knew who Kevin Durant was. People who did watch basketball now knew Wanda Durant, and they had an appreciation for what she'd done to help her son become a superstar.

Durant may not have intended it, but his public praise turned Wanda into a media sensation. Not only did media outlets reach out to interview her about her life, but she also became sought after as a motivational speaker. To this point, she had been an inspiration to her children. Now she was becoming an inspiration to others.

Lifetime television even made a movie about

her—*The Real MVP: The Wanda Durant Story.*

The Real MVP first aired on Lifetime in May 2016. Coincidentally, that was also the last time Kevin Durant would don an Oklahoma City Thunder uniform.

On May 30, 2016, Durant and the Thunder faced the Golden State Warriors in a deciding Game 7 of the NBA Western Conference Finals. The winner would play LeBron James and the Cleveland Cavaliers for the NBA championship title.

Durant had reached the NBA Finals in 2012, and though he'd been a force in that series—averaging thirty-one points per game—the Thunder had lost in five games to the Miami Heat. Durant desperately wanted to get back to the finals. Unfortunately for Durant and the Thunder, the Warriors were too much for them in Game 7.

Before Durant had much time to decompress from the hard-fought series with the Warriors, it was on to the next big story: Durant was a free agent. Would he stay with the Thunder or sign else-where?

Fans and the media spent the month of June speculating about what Durant would do. Wanda, along with many other family members and friends from the Maryland area, was hoping he would come back home and play for the Washington Wizards. But to almost everyone's surprise, Durant announced to the world on July 4, 2016, that he was signing with the Golden State Warriors.

Wanda might have been hoping that he would opt for the Wizards, but she never tried to persuade her son to do anything he didn't want to do. And when Durant started receiving harsh criticism for his decision to join what was already considered the best team in basketball, she came running to his defense.

Wanda became a regular on sports TV and radio talk shows once again, and she had strong words for anyone who questioned Kevin's motives.

ESPN broadcaster Stephen A. Smith called Durant's move from Oklahoma City to Golden State "the weakest move" in NBA history. When asked about that on another ESPN show during the 2017 NBA Finals, Wanda fired back.

"I thought that was quite harsh," she said. "Who are you, Stephan A., to come at my boy like that? . . . When he [Stephen A. Smith] came to ESPN, was that a weak move for him? He joined some more heavy hitters, right? To up his career, to do what was best for him. . . . No one called him weak for that. So why call my son weak for doing the same thing he did?"

A few days later the Warriors clinched the championship. Durant was named NBA Finals MVP, and the national TV audience saw him get to celebrate with his mom.

"To experience this with her . . . She knows how important it is to me," said Durant. "It's something we will be talking about for the rest of our lives."

CHAPTER 7

THE UNICORN

Taras Brown, who had started as Durant's AAU coach but had grown to become so much more in his life, had often given young Kevin inspirational and motivational quotes to put him into the proper frame of mind. Durant's favorite quote was this one:

"Hard work beats talent when talent fails to work hard."

When Durant was young, he didn't think he had the natural talent that so many others have seen in him, but that was a good thing because it made him work.

"My thing was I had an appropriate fear," Durant said. "Like, I knew if I didn't go to the gym that I wasn't going to be able to perform the right way. Or that next game I wouldn't be able to go out there and produce if I didn't work on my game."

Quinn Cook, one of a handful of players from PG County who also made it to the NBA, recalled his early impressions of Durant.

"When I met [Kevin], he wasn't the best in the city or anything," Cook said in October 2017 when he signed a ten-day contract with the Warriors, briefly reuniting with Durant. "He was just a tall kid who could shoot, but you could see his work ethic. You just saw him every day getting better and better. He taught me how to really work."

What makes Durant such a special player is that he works hard and has unique talent.

Taras Brown actually thought that some of Durant's talent was a direct result of the world around him when he was a child. Basketball coaches talk about the importance of "court awareness"—always knowing what's going on around you on the court. Durant had to grow up with street awareness, and Brown thinks that helped his game.

"You have to be instinctive in a neighborhood like that," Brown said. "You always have to have your head on a swivel. You have to know what's going on around you, because you can be walking down the street, and then something could be happening."

Brown is convinced that this made Durant's basketball instincts better, that it helped him make quick decisions and see things before they happened. Of course, the other part of growing up in this stressful environment was that it put the pressure of playing basketball into perspective.

"He used to say to me, 'There's nothing I see on the court that I'm afraid of,' because what he saw on a day-to-day basis in the neighborhood was much worse. On the court there's no pressure. This should be fun, and it is fun to him."

The combination of hard work, natural talent, and instincts have made him a dominant basketball player.

"When I watch him play the game, it's incredible to see how he puts it all together," said Steve Nash, a two-time NBA MVP who has been working with the Golden State Warriors as a player development consultant. "His size and skill set is something we've never really seen in this league. We've seen very skilled big guys before, tall guys, but not with his combination of size, skill, athleticism, agility, quickness, ability to play multiple positions, and to be as accurate as he is."

His ability goes back to his AAU days, when Coach Brown pushed him to play different positions and not be limited to playing the post, which is what most big men do. Playing on the perimeter helped him become a better dribbler, passer, and shooter. Of course, his height is a big advantage, as is his wingspan—when he extends his arms to either side, the measurement is an incredible seven feet, four inches, from his left fingertips to his right fingertips. That wingspan helps him pull down rebounds, make easy layups and dunks, and block shots.

"I don't think there's been a Kevin Durant. Ever," said former NBA player and current coach Doc Rivers. "I don't think there's ever been a comparison. . . . I don't think in the years that I've coached and played … there's ever been a more difficult guy to prepare for. You really feel like you're wasting your time doing it. He's going to probably score anyway."

While Durant can do many different things on the court, scoring points is still his specialty. And the reason he's such a scoring threat is because he can do it in so many different ways—driving to the basket, shooting from long distance, or using his great wingspan to make a mid-range jumper look easy.

Not only has he led the NBA four times in scoring, he's never averaged fewer than twenty points a game in any one season. In fact, his rookie season (when he averaged just over twenty points per game) was the only season in which he averaged fewer than twenty-five points per game.

Through the first eleven seasons of his career, Durant averaged 27.12 points per game—ranking him fifth in NBA history. The three players ranked at the top are all Hall of Famers—Michael Jordan (30.12 points per game), Wilt Chamberlain (30.07), and Elgin Baylor (27.36). In fourth place, just a fraction ahead of Durant with a 27.15 average, is LeBron James.

Having now faced off against Durant in the NBA Finals three times, James understands Durant's greatness as well as anyone else does.

"He's a seven-footer with six-footer ball-handling skills and a jump shot," James once said of Durant. "And athleticism. It's never been done in our league. We never had a guy that was seven feet that can jump like that, that can shoot like that, that can handle the ball like that. So it sets him apart."

Again, it all goes back to Durant's work ethic.

Coach Brown always tells people that Durant never likes to leave the court, whether it's practice or a game. He always wants to know what he can do better, wants to make sure he's doing everything right and always giving it his all. Brown recalled that even on off-days, Durant would contact him and ask about something having to do with basketball.

"I work so hard. I work tirelessly," Durant explained in the documentary *Still KD: Through the Noise.*

"What you don't see, that's the stuff that matters. That's what the kids need to know. I just keep building on that foundation I laid down twenty years ago."

Nash, who played with and against so many NBA superstars during his twenty-year career, has struggled when trying to find the right way to describe Durant's unique ability.

"Kids are saying he's a unicorn," said Nash. "I'll go with that!"

CHAPTER 8

TALL TALES

When Kevin Durant was in the second grade, his favorite NBA player was Grant Hill. He even had a Grant Hill jersey.

But as he got a little older, he had a new favorite player. And there was a very specific reason.

When Durant was eight years old, the Toronto Raptors used their first-round pick in the 1997 NBA Draft to get a six-foot-eight high school kid named Tracy McGrady. After three good years with the Raptors, McGrady signed with the Orlando Magic, and he blossomed into one of the best players in the league. McGrady made the all-star game seven times and twice led the league in scoring.

One of the things that made McGrady so valuable was that he could play both guard and forward. While height is an important quality for forwards, you don't see too many six-foot-eight athletes playing guard, a position that requires more quickness and ball handling. McGrady made it look easy, and Durant—even as a kid—could appreciate a taller athlete who refused to be stuck in one position because of his height.

"I tried to follow his moves, his energy on the court," Durant once said. "Just how he played, how he reacted to things. We had similar body types. Being a guy that can shoot at this height, I tried to emulate him as much as I could."

Durant was always self-conscious about his height—and his mother knew it. Wanda Durant used to ask the teachers to mix things up whenever they had to line up their students. Kids in school are used to lining up in size order—so naturally Durant was always last in line. Wanda asked them to mix it up and occasionally line up with the tallest in front, or not by size order at all, so that Kevin wasn't always stuck in the back.

Durant's grandmother Barbara also knew he was self-conscious about his height. She told Durant that one day he would see that being so tall was a blessing. She was right, of course, but it took a while.

When Durant played AAU basketball, Wanda had to make sure that her son's coaches always had Kevin's birth certificate handy. AAU can be very competitive, and it's not uncommon for teams to sometimes sneak in "ringers"—older kids who should not be on the roster.

Because Durant was so much taller than the other kids his age, AAU opponents always thought he was a ringer.

By the time Durant finished his freshman year

of high school, he was six foot eight—the same height as McGrady when he entered the NBA.

To this day, Kevin Durant's profile page on NBA. com lists his height as six feet, nine inches. Don't believe it.

Durant was six foot nine at some point in his life—maybe in college—but a lot of people have doubted that height listing since he entered the NBA. In the summer of 2016, USA Basketball released a team photo that showed Durant standing next to center and power forward DeMarcus Cousins, who is listed as six foot eleven. It seemed clear that Durant was taller than Cousins.

Speculation has been that Durant was a little sensitive about his height, though not for the reasons why he was self-conscious about it as a kid. In the NBA there are plenty of players his height. The sensitivity now was mainly because of the basketball perception. It's so uncommon for a player taller than six foot nine to be anything but a center or power forward. Durant preferred to play small forward, a position that requires more versatility and allows you to score in different ways, not just making layups and dunks from under the basket. So the speculation was that Durant thought more people would accept him as a small forward if he were six foot nine.

For whatever reason, he finally came clean during his first season with the Warriors.

"I was recorded at six ten and three-quarters with no shoes," Durant told KNBR radio on December 13, 2016. "So with my shoes on, I'm seven feet."

When asked why he never admitted that before, Durant replied: "I just like messin' with people."

When asked by the *Wall Street Journal* later that year, Durant had a little fun with it. "For me, when I'm talking to women, I'm seven feet," he said. "In basketball circles, I'm six nine."

CHAPTER 9

THE RIGHT DECISION

When a young Kevin Durant told his mother he wanted to play in the NBA, that was it.

"I didn't think I was going to be in the NBA, but I didn't plan on anything else since I was like nine," Durant said in the documentary *Still KD: Through the Noise*.

"I was humble enough to know that this may not happen, but I was arrogant enough to be like, 'I have no choice but to be.'"

In many ways Durant remained on a straight trajectory toward NBA stardom from that moment when he was eight years old right up until that fateful day in 2016 when he announced his intentions to sign a two-year, $54.3 million contract with the Golden State Warriors.

For all those years, Durant was focused not only on being the best basketball player he could be, but also on making everybody around him happy. Whether it was his family, his teammates, or his fans, he never wanted to let anyone down.

Which is why the reaction to his signing with the Warriors hurt him.

"It really pains me to know that I will disappoint so many people with this choice," Durant wrote on the Players' Tribune website when he announced the decision, "but I believe I am doing what I feel is the right thing at this point in my life and my playing career."

Durant was right about Thunder fans being disappointed, but they weren't the only ones. Many NBA fans and media members were critical of

Durant for signing with a stacked Warriors team that had just won seventy-three regular-season games and had been in the NBA Finals two years in a row.

The signing drew comparisons to LeBron James signing with the Miami Heat in the summer of 2010. LeBron James, Dwyane Wade, and Chris Bosh all signed with Miami, forming what the media called a "super team." Sure enough, the Heat went to four straight NBA Finals with the trio, and won the title twice.

Because Durant was joining a team that already had Stephen Curry, Klay Thompson, and Draymond Green, there was now immense pressure on Durant to help bring the NBA crown back to Golden State. With Durant in the lineup, the Warriors were viewed as heavy favorites to win it all. And some people thought Durant was taking the easy way out.

Those who know Durant best saw it differently.

They saw it as Durant finally doing something for himself.

"Kevin is a loving, generous, kind person," said his mother. "He's the kind of person that believes that everyone is inherently good. That's just how Kevin is. Since he moved teams to go to the Warriors from Oklahoma, people have said some really horrific things about him. It's been quite hurtful as his mom, but I said, 'Those people can't know Kevin.' Sometimes it's difficult because I don't understand why people don't just love him, because he's such a sweetheart. They really don't know him. Because to know him is to love him."

Michael Beasley, Durant's childhood friend and fellow NBA player, totally understood his friend's decision to play for the Warriors. He always saw Durant as someone who would sacrifice for others, always give the shirt off his back. So Beasley was happy that his friend had finally gotten to make a decision that Durant could enjoy.

"I'm looking at him wanting to play basketball, wholehearted basketball," Beasley said. "To where it's no pressure, but it's fun. The numbers is for everybody, shots is for everybody. Playing basketball the right way. But more than that, he made a decision to make himself happy, man. And I was so happy to see him do that."

Durant admitted that this was exactly the case. He understood that there are more responsibilities when you get older, but he longed for that carefree feeling he'd had when he was playing with Beasley on the PG Jaguars.

"Back then we had that," Durant said. "I want that kid-like feeling again for the game, and I wanted to try and duplicate that. And I was like, man, this is the perfect spot for me to play like we played with the Jaguars, you know what I'm saying? . . . I was just like, I need that feeling again."

Before donning the blue-and-gold jersey of the Golden State Warriors, there was one other team

Durant suited up for: the red, white, and blue of Team USA.

The 2016 summer Olympics in Rio de Janeiro, Brazil, was not the first time that Durant got to represent his country in international play, but it may have been the most meaningful. After all the criticism about his decision to sign with Golden State, Durant needed to get away. Rio was just what the doctor ordered.

"It was therapy for me after making a big change in my life," Durant told the Vertical after scoring thirty points in a 96–66 win over Serbia to clinch the gold medal. "It made my life easier. . . . I knew [a backlash] was coming. It was definitely different for me, but to come here in an environment where people accepted me and didn't care about anything except being my buddy, that's what I needed."

Durant started all eight games in the Olympics and was Team USA's leading scorer in three games. Among all players in the twelve-team tournament, he finished first in three-pointers (25) and second in total points (155).

"It was just an amazing time," Durant said. "We got together July 17, and we all set our minds on wearing one of these gold medals. That was our main focus."

Durant spoke of his love for the game, but it was clear that he was still hurt by the criticism he had been receiving back in the United States.

"I love the game so much. I started playing it because it was fun to me. I can't let anybody steal my joy," he said. "I get joy when I'm out there playing and it went to another level just playing alongside these great players and playing under Coach K [Team USA coach Mike Krzyzewski] and his staff. I focused on that. All that noise around me kind of quieted down. I just don't let anybody steal my joy and keep playing the game the way I know how to play it."

The 155 points that Durant scored in the 2016

Olympics was just one point shy of the USA Basketball record for most points scored in one Olympics. Who holds that record? Durant—he scored 156 points during the 2012 Olympics in London.

If he plays for Team USA in the 2020 Olympics in Tokyo, Durant would need just twenty-five more points to pass his good friend Carmelo Anthony and become the all-time leading American scorer in Olympics basketball history.

Typical of Durant, though, it's not the records or statistics that motivate him.

"You're playing for the whole country, and everybody's watching," he told *Sports Illustrated* before the 2016 games in Rio. "It's exciting. . . . It's a dream come true."

CHAPTER 10

BACK-TO-BACK

When the 2016–17 season began, Durant seemed to fit right in with the powerhouse Warriors. In just his second game with Golden State, he recorded thirty points and seventeen rebounds, which was one short of his career high for rebounds. In his third game he scored thirty-seven points. On November 3, in his first meeting against his former team, Durant made seven three-pointers and scored thirty-nine points in a 122–96 win over the Thunder.

The Warriors then cruised through the Western

Conference, and it seemed all but inevitable that they would meet the Cavs in the finals for a third straight year—a rubber match to crown a new NBA dynasty. Still, Durant continued to receive criticism for his decision to join Golden State.

"It's hard to make it to the top of your profession no matter what it is, but it's easy for people to discredit you," he said. "It's like, man, you worked your whole life to get to this point, and sometimes you don't even enjoy it because you're worried about what other people got to say. That's a struggle some days, especially when you're playing in the NBA, where all you hear is the noise. It's hard to tune it out."

But tune it out is exactly what he did. On February 11, 2017, he returned to Oklahoma City to play his first game there as a visiting player. He was booed loudly from the moment he stepped onto the court, and throughout the game. Still, he tuned out the noise and scored thirty-four points in a 130–114 win.

By the time his first regular season with the

Warriors was over, Golden State was the top seed in the playoffs. They cruised into the NBA Finals, winning twelve games in a row, setting up a third consecutive NBA Finals series against LeBron James and the Cleveland Cavaliers.

Back in the finals for the first time in five years, Durant was dominant. He was the team's leading scorer in the first two games, both victories. In addition to leading all players with thirty-three points and thirteen rebounds in Game 2, he added six assists, three steals, and five blocked shots. Golden State took a commanding 2–0 series lead.

"I'm just doing my job," Durant said on an off-day before heading to Cleveland for Game 3. "Doing what I was paid to do, which is to put in work, to get better no matter how I do it. Whether it's coming in early or waiting until after all the guys finish, and get my work in, I just gotta do it. I shouldn't be praised for doing what I'm supposed to be doing."

The Warriors played hard as Game 3 got under

way, and they had a hot hand from long range. Golden State set an NBA Finals record with twelve three-pointers in the first half, and led 67–61 at half-time. LeBron James and Kyrie Irving, however, led a furious Cleveland comeback in the second half. The Cavs' duo combined for seventy-seven points, and Cleveland was clinging to a 113–111 lead with less than a minute left.

That was when KD took matters into his own hands. After grabbing a defensive rebound, he dribbled down the court, defended by James. As Durant approached the three-point line, he pulled up and drilled the three-pointer that gave Golden State the lead for good. Durant finished with thirty-one points, and the Warriors won, 118–113.

"I've been working on that shot my whole life," Durant said after the game. "That was truly liberating. We need one more win. We've gotta keep going."

The Warriors were on the brink of becoming the first NBA team ever to make a perfect 16–0 run through the playoffs. As it turned out, the defending champs had too much pride to let that happen. The Cavaliers came out on fire in Game 4, scoring a record forty-six points in the first quarter and getting to eighty-six points by halftime. The game was also very chippy. Durant, who led the Warriors with thirty-five points, was not happy with some of the fouls he was taking. There was a lot of trash-talking, and at one point he and James got into each other's face. When the dust cleared, Cleveland had stayed alive with a 137–116 rout.

Just as Durant hadn't let the "noise" from fans and the media bother him during the season, he had no trouble shaking off the bad feelings of Game 4. The Warriors were denied their finals sweep, but they were determined to close out the series in Game 5— in front of their home crowd at Oracle Arena.

Cleveland jumped out to an early lead, but a Durant three-pointer gave Golden State a 45–43 lead with about ten minutes left in the first half.

James and Irving did their best to keep Cleveland in the game, and the Cavs pulled to within five points, heading into the fourth quarter. But Durant, with his first NBA title now so close that he could taste it, would not be denied.

Durant finished with thirty-nine points, including five three-pointers, as Golden State won, 129–120, to clinch the title.

"Another electrifying performance by Kevin Durant!" exclaimed Mike Breen on the ABC broadcast.

Indeed, KD was the Warriors' top scorer in all five games of the finals. He averaged 35.2 points, 8.4 rebounds, and 5.4 assists. As the last seconds of Game 5 ticked off, Durant had the ball in his hands. For the first time in his ten-year career, he could call himself an NBA champion.

Not only champion, though. With his overall performance, Durant was unanimously named the NBA Finals Most Valuable Player. He became just the third player in NBA history to have four scoring titles and an NBA championship on his résumé. The other two? Hall of Famers Michael Jordan and Wilt Chamberlain.

"I've achieved a lot of individual success in the league, and I'm proud of that, but it's nothing like winning it with your brothers, winning it for your city, as a team," Durant told the Warriors Radio Network after the Game 5 win. "Putting in the work every day, it's way bigger than myself. I couldn't do it, obviously, without my teammates, so they deserve a lot of credit.

"It's great to be a champion with these guys."

When Durant had first signed with the Warriors, he'd used some of his money to refurbish basketball courts in a low-income section of Oakland. At the court dedication he explained to the kids in attendance that he welcomes the opportunity to use his platform as a basketball player to help and inspire others.

"Being in the NBA is an amazing dream of mine. As a kid, that's all I wanted to do," he told them. "But as I got older, I realized the impact that we all have, as not only basketball players but as people to impact somebody's life. So to do this is my way of giving back and letting you guys know that the dream is always alive and always real. So always believe in yourself. That's what something as small as a basketball court did for me."

He wanted to make sure those kids understood that playing basketball with his friends was much more than just having fun. It taught him teamwork and leadership, positive qualities that can be applied to so much more than just basketball.

"All of those qualities, I learned while playing the game of basketball," he said. "So to be here, to see all of this come full circle, is a dream come true."

Durant had certainly displayed his teamwork and leadership abilities in his first season with the Warriors, which had culminated in his first NBA title.

In his second season with the Warriors, Golden State wasn't as dominant during the regular season. In fact, it was the Houston Rockets who finished with the best record. Nevertheless, the Warriors defeated Houston in the Western Conference Finals in a hard-fought seven-game series. Sure enough, the Warriors would face the Cavaliers in the NBA Finals for the fourth year in a row.

And unlike in 2017, when the Warriors missed pulling off the sweep by losing Game 4, this time they won four straight and broke out the brooms. And for the second straight year, Durant was named NBA Finals MVP.

Durant averaged 28.8 points in the series, along with 10.8 rebounds and 7.5 assists. His most memorable moment came in Game 3. He scored forty-three points in that contest, including a long three-pointer in the final minute, which sealed the win.

"Some of those shots, I don't think anybody in the world can hit those but him," Warriors coach Steve Kerr told the media after Game 3. "He was incredible.... His overall game tonight was ridiculous—the passing, the rebounding, the scoring. And it wasn't just the number of points. It was—it seemed like every time we needed a bucket, he got it for us."

Durant became the eleventh player in NBA history to be named finals MVP at least twice, and the other ten are all legendary figures in the sport: Michael Jordan, Magic Johnson, Shaquille O'Neal, Tim Duncan, LeBron James, Kobe Bryant, Larry Bird, Hakeem Olajuwon, Willis Reed, and Kareem Abdul-Jabbar.

He's the sixth player to win it in consecutive years—the others were Jordan, O'Neal, James, Olajuwon, and Bryant.

"Well deserved," Warriors star Stephen Curry said of Durant's MVP honor after Game 4. "The way he played all year, and especially in this final series, his Game 3 performance . . . so well deserved. . . . It's all about the ring. When KD looks back at those back-to-back finals MVPs, he'll remember all the guys that he suited up with and enjoyed that journey with. That's a great feeling to have."

Durant also talked about "the journey" in his postgame comments. He talked about how amazing it was to go to work every day with this group of players. He said that being around them helped him become not only a better basketball player but a better man.

"I've been working since I was eight years old to become a basketball player. That's all I wanted to do," he said. "To do it on this level, in the Finals, and be able to win a championship, it means a lot to me. But for our team it means so much. All the work we put in, the ups and downs, the injuries we persevered through. There's so much that we went through as a team. I'm happy we finished it up with a championship."

Just as he'd been taught at a young age to be a multidimensional player, Durant was proud to be more than just a scoring threat. He was glad to hear Coach Kerr praise his defense. And just because he was at the top of the NBA world, he wasn't ready to stop working.

"I feel like I'm at the peak of who I want to be, but I still have a lot of time to go," he said on the

TNT postgame show after Game 4. "A lot of places to get better at in my game. It's just exciting to know that I can affect the game in different ways. That's always been my goal since I was a kid. To do everything on the basketball court. And it's just amazing that Coach unlocked that for me, and my teammates encourage me to do everything."

The Warriors made the NBA Finals once again in 2019, but Durant's chance of winning an unprecedented third straight Finals MVP was derailed when he suffered a ruptured right Achilles tendon in Game 5 against the Toronto Raptors, who eventually won the title. Just a few weeks later, when Durant became a free agent, he announced that he would be signing with the Brooklyn Nets—a four-year deal worth $164 million. He would not be able to play for many months as he rehabilitated from the Achilles injury, but Durant would be starting a new chapter in his Hall of Fame career.

CHAPTER 11

BACK TO THE FUTURE

It might be hard to believe, but winning back-to-back NBA championships—and being named the NBA Finals MVP both times—did not change Kevin Durant. He remained the same good-natured, hardworking person he's been since the early days back in PG County.

"He's at the top and he hasn't changed anything, his character, what type of person he is," said Greivis Vásquez, a former teammate from Montrose Christian School who also went on to play in the NBA. "Sometimes you let that go to your head. But he knows his roots, where he came from. It's not easy being where he's at right now. Being one of the best, people expecting everything of you, but he's still doing it all the right way."

Durant knows his roots, and he hasn't let go of them. That's why, despite living across the country in Northern California, he makes it back to Seat Pleasant Activity Center as often as possible.

When the Warriors played at the Washington Wizards midway through the 2017–18 season, Durant invited a bunch of kids from the rec center to the game. Some even got to accompany the Warriors players who took a private tour of the Smithsonian National Museum of African American History and Culture.

Of course, many of these kids were already used to seeing Durant hanging around the rec center. In a story in *USA Today* during the 2018 NBA Finals, kids and staff at the rec center talked about how comfortable and laid-back Durant is whenever he visits.

Sometimes, related Taras Brown, Durant will stop by the rec center and just sit at the front desk to greet kids as they come in.

"He'll just sit there and watch them come in and if it's someone he knows he'll say, 'How'd you do in school this year? What are you doing, what are you up to?' Or a kid might come in that he knows and he's met the kid three or four times and the kid might come in and he might not say something to Kevin because the kid thinks, 'I wonder if Kevin remembers me?' So the kid comes in, scans his card, Kevin says, 'You're not going to speak to me?'"

Durant loves to visit the rec center, Brown said, and he's made a point of giving back to the center through generous donations. The rec center used to be closed on Sundays, but Durant donated money to help keep it open that day—"so the community could have another day to keep the kids off the street," said Brown.

As if anyone who visited Seat Pleasant Activity

Center wouldn't already know that Kevin Durant got his start there, replicas of his MVP ring and trophy sit on a table near the entrance.

"Kevin was always a role model here and someone who I looked up to," said Keith Shivers, who is about five years younger than Durant and had the opportunity to play against him a few times at the rec center.

Now, thanks to the international fame he has gained as an NBA superstar, Durant is able to be a role model not only to kids at the Seat Pleasant Activity Center, but also to kids around the world. Never forgetting where he came from, Durant has fully embraced that role.

In 2013, when he was still with the Oklahoma City Thunder, and a tornado ravaged the nearby town of Moore, Oklahoma, Durant donated one million dollars to the American Red Cross tornado disaster relief fund. And he used his platform to encourage Nike and the Thunder to match his donation.

Through the Kevin Durant Charity Foundation, the humble superstar is able to help kids all over. Its mission is "to enrich the lives of at-risk youth from low-income backgrounds through educational, athletic, and social programs."

In the summer of 2017, Durant took that mission to the international arena. Through the Kevin Durant Charity Foundation, he helped build and refurbish basketball courts for kids in India. The trip was in conjunction with the NBA, which has set up youth organizations to promote the sport of basketball in that country.

Working with the NBA, Durant made his way into the Guinness World Records, by hosting the largest basketball lesson ever. In a gym in New Delhi, Durant led basketball drills in front of eight hundred kids. That alone would have been the record, but there were another twenty-five hundred kids from nearby states in India participating via satellite.

Durant has had the good fortune to travel the world, and it has clearly given him perspective.

"Sometimes I feel small around people who experience much more than me," he said in a YouTube video chronicling his India trip. "So definitely trying to learn more and see different things, and this is a step . . . for me. So I'm excited."

Back in the States, he remains focused on the place where he grew up.

In February 2018, the Kevin Durant Charity Foundation made a ten-year, $10 million commitment to create the Durant Center, a new state-of-the-art educational and leadership facility in Prince George's County. Durant partnered on the project with College Track, whose mission is to empower students from underserved communities to graduate from college.

"This is the realization of a dream of mine," Durant said in announcing the plan. "To come back home and positively impact the lives of kids—who share the ambitions I've always had—with world-class educational opportunities and resources that can completely change the game in our community for generations to come."

The commitment is just an extension of who Kevin Durant has always been—that kid growing up in PG County who always wanted to please everyone. Even now that he has the ability to help others by simply donating money, that's not enough.

"I want you to know that I'm there," he said. "I want you to know that I really cared and I'm really genuine about it. Sometimes that doesn't come off well, especially with people of our stature that don't come around our communities a lot. But I want them to know that we still care, we're still there. We got our thing going on, but we're still part of our community emotionally, and that goes a long, long way, more so than what we can do from our pockets.

"For me that's something that I try to do every

single chance that I get. And on top of that, find creative ways to influence the community and elevate the community. Not just give money and move on. It's more of a life thing, and I think it's gonna help the kids down the line, help kids become something that they've always wanted to be."

For the kids who want to follow in Durant's footsteps, he created Team Durant—an AAU organization in the Maryland-DC area that features boys' and girls' basketball teams for kids from age nine to seventeen. Naturally, Taras Brown is involved.

"He wanted me to provide for others what we provided for him. He wanted kids to know there's more to life than Seat Pleasant, Maryland," said Brown. "He wanted youth basketball to affect other kids in this area, to help kids who may have been through what he's been through, or who saw what he saw. That's been our mission. We want the kids to learn and grow—not as basketball players but as young men."

Alan Stein, a basketball trainer who worked with Durant at Oak Hill Academy and then at Montrose Christian School, has remained close to Durant. He continues to marvel at Durant's work ethic and pure love of the game. But he's more impressed with Durant off the court.

"While the entire planet is aware of what an exceptional basketball player KD is, I have always been most proud of him as a person," Stein wrote in 2012 on USAB.com, the website for USA Basketball. "His character is unmatched. He is kind, generous, humble, and authentic. He is an exemplary role model in every sense of the word. His passion for the game is pure and his work ethic is unparalleled. He is the real deal."

Kevin Durant always wanted to be an NBA star, and through dedication and hard work that's what he has become.

He also wanted to be someone that people could rely on. That didn't take much hard work.

His generosity and kind heart came naturally. Part of it stemmed from his mother, whose love of her children was always in abundance. Part of it came from Charles Craig, the coach who would do anything for his kids at the rec center. Part of it came from Taras Brown, who was more than just a coach.

Most of it is just Kevin Durant, always learning from and improving on his experiences growing up in PG County.

SOURCES

Branch, John. "Behind Kevin Durant's Jersey Number, a Cold-Blooded Murder." *New York Times*, April 7, 2017. https://www.nytimes.com/2017/04/07/sports /basketball/kevin-durant-golden-state-warriors -jersey.html.

Cowan, Lee. "Wanda Durant, Kevin Durant's mother, opens up about sacrifice." CBS News, June 13, 2017. https://www.cbsnews.com/news/wanda-durant -kevin-durant-mother-real-mvp/.

Curry, Stephen. "Curry reacts to Durant winning second straight Finals MVP." NBC Sports video,

June 8, 2018. https://www.nbcsports.com/bayarea /video/curry-reacts-durant-winning-second-straight -finals-mvp.

Durant, Kevin. (@KDTray5). Twitter. https://twitter .com/KDTray5.

Durant, Kevin. "Kevin Durant: The Oklahoma City Thunder star's complete MVP speech." *The Oklahoman*, May 13, 2014. https://newsok.com /article/4815027/kevin-durant-the-oklahoma-city -thunder-stars-complete-mvp-speech.

Durant, Kevin. "Kevin Durant on Team USA Olympics 2016." Sports Illustrated video, July 19, 2016. https://www.youtube.com/watch?v=jI9zPgGUiA0.

Durant, Kevin. "KD Fan Q&A: On and Off the Court." YouTube video, January 12, 2018. https://www .youtube.com/watch?v=FRiVCKIpRaE.

Durant, Kevin. "My India Trip." YouTube video, August 3, 2017. https://www.youtube.com/watch?v=3o3chfNOdQ0.

Durant, Kevin. "My Next Chapter." The Players Tribune, July 4, 2016. https://www.theplayerstribune.com/en-us/articles/kevin-durant-nba-free-agency-announcement.

Durant, Kevin. "The Best Kevin Durant Quotations." Sports Feel Good Stories (website). https://www.sportsfeelgoodstories.com/kevin-durant-quotes/.

Durant, Wanda. "Kevin Durant's Mom Has Some Words for Stephen A. Smith." *First Take*, ESPN, ww v=DXyIbG9qcXc.

Durant, Wanda. *"Wanda Durant: the Real MVP."* Interview by Wendy Williams. *The Wendy Williams*

Show, Season 9, Episode 169, June 20, 2017. https://www.youtube.com/watch?v=UVvBRqG3aag.

"Former Texas assistant coach Russell Springmann tells us how he discovered Kevin Durant." *Mad Dog Sports Radio,* 2016.

Haynes, Chris. "Durant, Beasley open up about childhood friendship, NBA journey." ESPN.com, March 1, 2018. http://www.espn.com/nba/story/_/id /22606317/kevin-durant-michael-beasley-childhood -friendship-nba-journey.

Kevin Durant Charity Foundation, The. "Kevin Durant Charity Foundation, College Track & Prince George's County Public Schools Team Up To Empower Students Striving For College Success With Innovative Program & New Educational Facility." PR Newswire, February 27, 2018. https://www .prnewswire.com/news-releases/kevin-durant

-charity-foundation-college-track--prince-georges
-county-public-schools-team-up-to-empower
-students-striving-for-college-success-with
-innovative-program--new-educational-facility
-300604756.html.

"Kevin Durant / Charles Craig Special on ESPN—
2012 NBA Playoffs." *NBA Countdown*, ESPN, 2012.
https://www.youtube.com/watch?v=gQZahU_1cQo.

Kogod, Sarah. "Kevin Durant shows the world where
he came from." *Washington Post*, July 1, 2013. https
://www.washingtonpost.com/news/dc-sports-bog
/wp/2013/07/01/kevin-durant-shows-the-world
-where-he-came-from/?utm_term=.4b613a857ba1.

Lee, Michael. "KD on Team USA experience: 'It
was therapy for me.'" Yahoo! Sports, August 22,
2016. https://sports.yahoo.com/news/kd-team-usa
-experience-therapy-000000944.html.

Letourneau, Connor. "Quinn Cook reunites with 'big brother' Kevin Durant on Warriors." *San Francisco Chronicle*, October 28, 2017. https://www.sfgate.com /warriors/article/Quinn-Cook-reunites-with-big -brother-Kevin-12309964.php.

Still KD: Through the Noise. Directed by Brandon Loper. Released July 11, 2017. Documentary, YouTube video. https://www.youtube.com/watch?v=l_2IwlwayG8.

Maese, Rick. "Kevin Durant, the NBA's unassuming superstar, remembers his D.C. roots." *Washington Post*, February 24, 2012. https://www.washingtonpost .com/sports/wizards/kevin-durant-the-nbas -unassuming-superstar-remembers-his-dc-roots /2012/02/24/gIQAQpB8XR_story.html?utm_term =.c5c6bd19515c.

Mandell, Nina. "Kevin Durant inspires next generation of 'rec center kids' with another title."

USA Today Sports, June 9, 2018. https://ftw.usatoday
.com/2018/06/kevin-durant-seat-pleasant-nba
-mvp-warriors.

Mandell, Nina. "Kevin Durant says he's 7 feet
tall, but only when talking to women." USA
Today Sports, May 4, 2016. https://ftw.usatoday
.com/2016/05/kevin-durant-height-thunder.

Mayberry, Darnell. "Why 35? The story behind a jersey
number and Kevin Durant's devotion to his coach."
The Oklahoman, March 24, 2010. https://newsok.com
/article/3448737/why-35-the-story-behind-a-jersey
-number-and-kevin-durants-devotion-to-his-coach.

Moore, Matt. "The great debate is over: Warriors'
Kevin Durant finally admits his real height." CBS
Sports, December 17, 2016. https://www.cbssports
.com/nba/news/the-great-debate-is-over-kevin
-durant-finally-admitted-his-real-height/.

Morsy, Sam. "LeBron praises KD: He's a 7-footer with 6-foot ball-handling skills." The Score, December 17, 2015. https://www.thescore.com/nba/news/913409.

Picker, David. "In the NBA's Age Game, Colleges Are Big Winners." *New York Times*, April 22, 2006. https://www.nytimes.com/2006/04/22/sports /in-the-nbas-age-game-colleges-are-big-winners .html.

Stein, Alan. "15 Things You Can Learn from Kevin Durant." USA Basketball (website), April 13, 2012. https://www.usab.com/youth/news/2012/04/15 -things-you-can-learn-from-kevin-durant.aspx.

"Taras Brown, Durant's Mentor, Godfather & Coach, Opens Up About KD." *Warrior's Huddle*, podcast, January 20, 2017. http://www.blogtalkradio.com /warriors-huddle/2017/01/21/taras-brown-durants -mentor-godfather-coach-opens-up-about-kd.

2017 NBA Finals, Game 3, postgame coverage on TNT, June 12, 2017.

2018 NBA Finals, Game 3, postgame press conference on ABC, June 6, 2018.

"U.S. Olympic Men's Basketball Team Claims Third Straight Gold With 96–66 Rout of Serbia." USA Basketball (website), August 21, 2016. https://www.usab.com/news-events/news/2016/08/moly-vs-srb-gold-medal-recap.aspx.

ABOUT THE AUTHOR

Craig Ellenport is a sports journalist who has written more than a dozen books. During his thirty-year career he has covered the NBA, the NFL, the NHL, MLB, college football, and tennis.

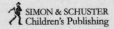